ELOQUENT TRIBUTES

TASNIM BENSACI

Copyright © 2024 by Tasnim Bensaci.

All rights reserved. No part of this publication may be reproduced, distributed, or transmitted in any form or by any means, including photocopying, recording, or other electronic or mechanical methods, without the written consent of the publisher. The only exceptions are for brief quotations included in critical reviews and other noncommercial uses permitted by copyright law.

MILTON & HUGO L.L.C.
4407 Park Ave., Suite 5
Union City, NJ 07087, USA

Website: *www. miltonandhugo.com*
Hotline: *1- 888-778-0033*
Email: *info@miltonandhugo.com*

Ordering Information:
Quantity sales. Special discounts are granted to corporations, associations, and other organizations. For more information on these discounts, please reach out to the publisher using the contact information provided above.

Library of Congress Control Number:	IN-PROCESS
ISBN-13: 979-8-89285-042-1	[Paperback Edition]
979-8-89285-043-8	[Digital Edition]

Rev. date: 02/12/2024

Scripting The Soul
A Journey Through Words

I felt if I didn't write nobody would accept me as a being. Writing, then, is a substitute for myself: if you don't love me, love my writing and love me for my writing. Where shadows linger and whispers of emptiness echo, there exists a yawning chasm, gaping wide with the absence of words. Life bereft of writing is a desolate landscape, where the sun refuses to cast its warming rays, and the moon mourns in silver tears for the lost artistry of expression. My pen, a faithful companion in this odyssey of existence, holds within its slender form more than mere ink; it cradles the weight of untold secrets, the echoes of unspoken truths, and the fervent whispers of a restless spirit.

Without the alchemy of language to sculpt the raw clay of thought into something tangible, I am but a ghost drifting through the corridors of time, faceless and forgotten. For it is through the medium of writing that I find sanctuary, where the tumultuous waves of identity crash against the sturdy cliffs of prose, shaping me into something more than flesh and bone, more than mere existence.

To write is to unravel the enigma of self, to peel back the layers of uncertainty and reveal the pulsing heart of purpose that beats beneath. Each stroke of the pen is a brushstroke upon the canvas of my soul, painting a portrait of resilience and defiance in the face of oblivion. For in the act of creation, I forge my own identity, a beacon of light in the suffocating darkness of anonymity.

I am born to be a writer, destined to navigate the labyrinthine corridors of the human experience, to plumb the depths of emotion and ascend to the dizzying heights of imagination. In the tapestry of existence, I am but a single thread, yet woven with such intricacy and finesse that I defy the hands of time to unravel me.

There is history to be read, vast and sprawling like the heavens themselves, waiting to be deciphered by the hungry mind of the seeker. Each word a breadcrumb leading deeper into the labyrinth, each sentence a signpost guiding me toward enlightenment. And so I read, voracious in my hunger for knowledge, insatiable in my thirst for understanding.

But beyond the confines of the written word lies a world teeming with mysteries waiting to be unravelled, each person a puzzle to be solved, each passion a flame to be ignited. And in the act of discovery, I find solace, for I am not alone in my quest for meaning.

—In ink I find my essence, words my refuge in a world of silence. Through writing, I unveil my soul, seeking acceptance not for my form but for the stories I unfold.

Daughter

In the realm of boyhood, our household resembled a vibrant canvas adorned with immigrant tales—stitched with expectations and echoes that clung to the walls. As a daughter navigating this mosaic, I found myself akin to a solitary note in a boisterous symphony of masculine voices, a delicate harmony set against the robust melodies around me. The kitchen, fragrant with the spice-laden whispers of ancestral stories, became a realm where I stitched together my identity, threading the delicate balance between heritage and societal norms.

In this dynamic choreography, akin to dancing between immigrant dreams and cultural expectations, I found myself forging a path uniquely mine. The household, akin to a crucible of diverse echoes, witnessed my journey—a daughter grappling with unspoken rules, reshaping the narrative as I bore the weight of familial expectations. Growing up in an all-boy environment was akin to navigating a thicket, where resilience became my shield and grace my guide, much like a solitary bloom amidst towering oaks.

The pressure on my shoulders manifested like a burdensome burden, akin to balancing an intricate sculpture with fragile fragments. It was a delicate act of equilibrium, a metaphorical juggling of diverse elements within an intricate dance. The weight of familial expectations became a tangible force, much like Atlas shouldering the world, and in that delicate balance, I learned the art of resilience amidst societal pressures. This household, an arena of contrasting melodies and expectations, became a space where my unique song echoed—a melody forged through the crucible of an immigrant narrative, resonating with both strength and grace.

—I am the solitary bloom amidst towering oaks, navigating a path of resilience amidst echoes of expectations.

Tribute To Sisterhood

Women unfold like the delicate petals of a blossoming flower, each connection a vibrant hue weaving a masterpiece of sisterhood. Our bonds are akin to the gentle dance of leaves in a sunlit forest, swaying in harmonious rhythms, embracing the diversity of our stories and experiences. Like a symphony of laughter echoing through the valleys, our camaraderie resonates with the joyous melodies of shared secrets and unspoken understanding. In the garden of friendship, we are seeds planted side by side, growing into a lush, interconnected oasis, where roots intertwine, offering support in both storm and sunlight. Our sisterhood is a sanctuary, a constellation of stars guiding each other through the vast, sometimes tumultuous, skies of life. Together, we are an unyielding force, a testament to the enduring beauty and freedom found in the sacred heart of our collective journey. In the enchanting tableau of our lives, the bonds between women blossom with the timeless elegance of a carefully choreographed waltz in a ballroom bathed in soft, sepia-toned light. Our friendships, dear as a cherished vintage photograph, capture the essence of an era where the strength of sisterhood echoed through the decades. Picture us as pages in a classic novel, each turning moment revealing the resilience and grace, our unity mirroring the steady hum of a well-tuned jukebox playing melodies that resonate in the heart. Our conversations, like letters penned with quill and ink, are steeped in the honesty of a bygone era, where authenticity is the currency of our connection.

—In the sacred grove of sisterhood, women unfurl like ethereal petals, each a masterpiece in the tapestry of camaraderie.

Intellectum

In the delicate dance of beauty's gaze, a quiet narrative unfurls, veiled by assumptions and misconceptions. Beneath the facade of allure lies a mind, a repository of thoughts unexplored. Yet, in the echo chambers of perception, doubts sprout like unbidden weeds—seeds of scepticism sown by a world quick to dismiss intellect beneath a veneer of beauty. A paradox unfolds, where the allure becomes both a shield and a cage, trapping the depth within.

In the realm of pretty faces, the intellect often becomes an overlooked terrain, dismissed as a mere backdrop to a captivating visage. Whispers of doubt linger, casting shadows on the validity of thoughts that strive to transcend the surface. Conversations become a battlefield, where every word is measured against the preconceived notion that beauty and intelligence stand in contradiction.

Yet, within the silence, a resilience blossoms—an unyielding force to challenge the status quo. Thoughts, like delicate petals, unfurl despite the persistent doubt. The struggle to be heard, to be taken seriously, becomes a poignant refrain—a melody of intellect eclipsed by a society's narrow gaze.

In the hallowed halls of perception, the journey to break free from the confines of stereotype is a symphony of perseverance.

Like a rare bloom, intelligence becomes a subtle revelation, emerging from the soil of assumptions. For in the quiet corridors of understanding, the truth unfolds—a testament that beauty and intellect can harmonise, a melody drowned out by the clamour of disbelief.

—In beauty's gaze, intellect hides its depth, a silence obscured by societal misconceptions. Yet within the quiet of understanding, truth blooms—a harmonious fusion of beauty and intellect, defying disbelief's clamour.

Silent Strength
The Veiled Narrative

Within the quiet drape of fabric, I embrace the journey of veiling. navigating the nuanced currents of perception. Society's gaze weaves a complex judgement around me, casting shadows on the layers that enshroud my identity. Beyond the threads lies a narrative, often misconstrued, a story of resilience silently carried within.

The veil, more than mere cloth, is a symbol of my endurance—a canvas on which societal biases are painted. The world looks upon me through a lens distorted by stereotypes, rendering my silent struggles invisible. Yet, beneath these modest folds, I carry the weight of history—a history written in every stitch, woven with threads of faith and conviction.

To veil is not an act of submission but a declaration of my autonomy, a defiance against a world that often seeks to define me. Society, with its judgmental eyes, may attempt to confine me within narrow constraints, but I emerge unyielding—a symbol of resilience and hope.

In each moment of veiling, I wrap myself in the armour of my beliefs, a shield against the storms of ignorance. The modest attire becomes my declaration of identity, a testament to the strength that lies within. Through the gaze of society, I transcend, a silhouette against a backdrop of misunderstanding.

My journey, a quiet rebellion against the stereotypes that seek to imprison me, unfolds like the unfurling petals of a delicate flower. Veiling becomes my act of self-expression, a dance with the wind, a whisper against societal cacophony.

In the tapestry of veiling, I stitch stories of courage and resilience, crafting a narrative that transcends the surface. The veil, not a shroud of oppression, but a beacon of hope—a reminder that my strength is often found in the folds of what is unseen.

— I navigate this journey, unseen struggles concealed beneath societal judgments. The veil, more than cloth, symbolises endurance—a canvas where biases paint a distorted portrait.

Innocence's Undoing

Within the folds of memory, a delicate thread unravels, revealing a narrative stained with the premature loss of innocence. A child, adorned in hues of trust, encountered shadows—a cruel and unjust gust that altered the course of her tender journey. Laughter, the natural bloom of youth, gave way to echoes that cast shadows, leaving behind a sombre gloom in the corners of recollection.

In this sanctuary meant for joy, a story unfolded—a narrative etched with the deepest scars, where the world's cruelty met the vulnerability of a child beneath the moon and stars. The innocence, once a tender petal, became stained by a touch that left the soul deeply wounded, a secret whispered in the silence of night, where darkness veiled the torment, shrouded from the world's gaze.

The river of time attempts to conceal, but the ripples of anguish persist, emotions unrevealed in the realms of memory where shadows dance. A child's whispered agony echoes, creating a painful trance that refuses to be muted by the passing of time.

Yet, even within the sadness, a semblance of beauty may be found—a resilience emerging like a soft, rising tide. In the broken places, there's a strength to reclaim, a survivor's spirit that, though forever changed, refuses to be wholly defined by the scars.

In the journey of healing, a story unfolds—a wounded child, gradually moulding strength. Through tears and the echoes of silent cries, emerges a beauty, resilient beneath sorrowful skies. May the echoes find solace as healing begins, embraced by the gentle passage of time, where compassion emerges victorious.

"I was just a child; how could I have known better?" A refrain that echoes through the narrative, a plea for understanding woven into the fabric of a painful reality. The story unfolds, revealing the complexities of innocence lost, yet within the sadness, a glimmer appears—a testament to strength as a wounded soul perseveres.

— a fragile narrative unravels, innocence tarnished by premature loss. Laughter fades to shadows, leaving a sombre echo in the corners of recollection, where a child's trust met the world's cruelty beneath the moon's watchful eye.

Revenge

In contemplation, I expounded upon the perilous allure of revenge, the hazardous luxury embedded within the realms of hate and malice. I reflected on the profound truth that, even when malice and venom appear to be 'richly deserved,' the indulgence in these emotions, alas, proves to be ruinous. The areas of a lady's imagination, remarkably swift, leaps from admiration to love, and in a mere moment, transcends into the realm of matrimony. I find myself disabused of all faith, the clarity of disillusionment shaping my perspective. Amidst the intricate mosaic of emotions, there exist select individuals whom I cherish, though their number is limited. My commitment to a dogged and inexplicable sense of dignity persists, an unwavering integrity that demands preservation. Having traversed a considerable distance relying on trust funds, I now find myself bankrupt in that particular line, grappling with the implications of this newfound financial and metaphorical insolvency.

—In introspection, I pondered the treacherous allure of revenge, the perilous path embedded in hate's embrace. Reflecting on the harsh truth that indulging in malice proves ruinous, even when seemingly justified.

Lost Laughter

In the desolate corridors of my memories, there lingers the ghostly echo of a childhood lost, a spectral lament for innocence prematurely shattered. I was a fragile bud, forced to blossom too soon, burdened with the weight of traumas too heavy for a tender heart to bear. Like a wilting flower robbed of its chance to bloom, my laughter became a muted dirge, drowned in the dissonance of a world that demanded I grow beyond my years. Time, a cruel thief, stole the idyllic landscapes of carefree days and replaced them with the harsh terrain of premature responsibility.

I walked the path of adulthood while still a child, the shadows of innocence dissipating like morning dew under a relentless sun. My playgrounds transformed into battlegrounds, where the whimsical melodies of youth were silenced by the cacophony of harsh realities. Each step felt like an arduous journey, burdened by the weight of a stolen childhood, like an aged soul trapped within a fragile frame. Now, as an adult, I wander through the ruins of my past, a broken archaeologist seeking the remnants of my lost youth.

In my pursuit to reclaim the stolen fragments of joy, I grasp at elusive echoes, chasing the wistful spectres of laughter that once danced freely. Like a sailor yearning for a distant shore, I navigate the turbulent seas of adulthood, fueled by an insatiable desire to resurrect the child within me. Yet, the scars of a prematurely weathered heart persist, like a haunting melody that refuses to fade. In this bittersweet odyssey, I strive to rebuild the sandcastles of my shattered innocence, yearning to rediscover the childlike wonder stolen by the callous hands of time

— Time, a cruel thief, stole the landscapes of carefree days, leaving in their wake the harsh terrain of responsibility.

Desolation's Symphony

poverty painted our days with hues of melancholy, a canvas marked by the scarcity of coins and the echoes of hunger. Our family, a constellation of dreams tethered to empty pockets, scavenged for stray coins within the hollow echoes of our once-hopeful home, an impoverished orchestra seeking a symphony in the jingle of meagre coins. Milk, a luxury, became a whispered prayer at the altar of empty pockets, the stark reminder of a childhood spent in the desolation of financial despair.

We sought refuge in the distant west, chasing the elusive promise of a better life, only to find ourselves ensnared in the unforgiving web of hardship and challenge. Like nomads adrift in an arid expanse, our dreams withered under the unrelenting sun of adversity. The West, once an emblem of hope, transformed into a desolate wilderness, where the winds of despair swept away our aspirations like fragile sandcastles.

In the crucible of poverty, our family became alchemists of survival, transmuting tears into tales of endurance, and longing into a haunting lullaby. Our struggles etched a narrative of resilience on the walls of our humble abode, a dwelling worn thin by the weight of unmet aspirations. The westward journey, once painted with dreams, became a sombre pilgrimage, where hardship was the only currency we could not escape.

Yet, amidst the poignant echoes of hardship, the ache of empty pockets, and the relentless winds of misfortune, we clung to the fragments of hope, like mournful notes in a requiem. Our journey, a sorrow-laden odyssey, unfolded like chapters in a tragic novel, where the promise of a better life dissolved into the tear-stained pages of our collective history.

—our days were a symphony of scarcity, dreams echoing hollow.

Illumination

In the hall of mirrors, I danced a melancholy waltz with distorted reflections, a symphony of longing for the elusive beauty dictated by societal whims. My once-luscious locks, like strands of sorrow, clung to the bitter truth that beauty was an ephemeral wisp, slipping through fingers yearning for an unattainable allure. Society, a relentless sculptor, moulded my perception, each twist of its chisel carving away at the essence of self-love. Lips that were meant to speak volumes became a canvas for insecurities painted by the ever-changing standards of a fickle world.

The media, an unrelenting maestro, conducted a dissonant orchestra of conflicting ideals—today, be waif-like, tomorrow, embrace curves. Like a puppet in this beauty pageant, my reflection in the mirror became a haunting adversary, a canvas daubed with the brushstrokes of inadequacy. The teenage years, a tender chapter in the story of self-discovery, morphed into a landscape of thorns, each societal expectation a needle pricking at the canvas of my self-esteem.

The chase for beauty unfolded like a tragic ballet, my body pirouetting through the merciless critiques of societal gaze. I shed tears that glittered like crushed diamonds, remnants of a shattered perception of self-worth. Yet, within this shadowed narrative, I embarked on a clandestine journey—one of self-acceptance, each step a bruised but determined shuffle towards the oasis of inner beauty.

Finally, I discovered that beauty was not a reflection in the merciless mirrors of societal standards but an illumination from within.I embraced the scars, both visible and unseen. The dance with my reflection transformed into a graceful ballet of self-love, a testament to resilience in the face of a beauty-obsessed world. In the end, the saddest verses birthed a triumphant ode, and the mirror, once a foe, became a portal to the unfiltered beauty I found within myself.

—distorted images swayed to a mournful rhythm, yearning for an ideal beauty dictated by society's caprice. Moulded by unyielding standards, each stroke of perception eroded self-affection, leaving silenced lips and painted insecurities.

A Decades Dance

There was a chapter, a decade-long melody of friendship that resonated like a cherished ballad. For ten years, we danced through life's labyrinth hand in hand, our laughter intertwining like vines, creating an inseparable bond. We were more than friends; we were sisters of the heart, sharing secrets as sacred as whispers in the night. Each day was a symphony of shared moments, a sanctuary where our souls found solace in the other's company. She wasn't just a friend; she was the echo of my spirit.

Our bond, like an ancient oak, weathered storms together, standing resilient against the winds of time. I opened my home to her, and my mother, in her infinite kindness, welcomed her as kin. She became a part of our daily lives, her presence an indelible stroke in the canvas of our shared existence. We navigated the highs and lows, building a fortress of trust and understanding, a refuge against the world's uncertainties.

Yet, abruptly, the narrative of our sisterhood unravelled, a sweater unravelling at the seams. It was as if the symphony had been silenced, leaving behind echoes of laughter and shared secrets in the corridors of memory. Losing her was akin to a garden stripped of its blooms, a desolate landscape where the vibrant colours of companionship faded into grayscale. A part of me crumbled like ancient ruins, and the void left by her absence echoed with the hollowness of a fractured melody.

In the silence that followed, the rooms of my heart felt empty, haunted by the echoes of our laughter that once painted the walls with warmth. The home that embraced her now echoed with the poignant loneliness of separation. Our shared secrets, once safely guarded, became ghosts that lingered in the shadows, reminders of a friendship that was now but a melancholic echo in the recesses of time.

—the echoes of our connection lingered in the emptiness of Seperation.

Night Terror

In the shadowed realms of my restless nights, I confront the haunting spectre of a past that stains the canvas of my dreams. At the tender age of four, innocence shattered like fragile glass, and a malevolent touch etched its indelible mark upon my soul. Night terrors unfurl like ominous banners, nightmares like ghostly apparitions that dance in the corridors of my mind. His touch, an unwanted tattoo upon the canvas of my vulnerability, whispers cruel echoes through the corridors of time.

I was but a little girl, a budding flower in the garden of youth, not the architect of this heart-wrenching script. The burden of shame, a cloak unjustly thrust upon fragile shoulders, weighed heavy. Yet, as I grew, an alchemist in the crucible of resilience, I forged strength from the shards of my broken innocence. I learned to forgive the child I once was, for innocence lost is not a choice but a stolen treasure.

His touch, a phantom limb, seeks refuge in the recesses of my memory, yet I rise from the embers of despair. I carved a sanctuary within, a fortress adorned with self-love and defiance. Brave expressions bloom like flowers in the aftermath of a storm, each word a testament to the unwavering spirit that refuses to be silenced.

I am not defined by the shadows that linger in the corners of my past. I am a symphony of survival, a melody of strength rising from the cacophony of a violated silence. In the mirror, I find an affirmation of self-love, a reflection of resilience staring back. I am a warrior who has faced the darkest of nights, embraced the wounded inner child, and emerged adorned with the armour of forgiveness.

My story unfolds, a narrative of bold reclamation. For I am not a victim; I am a survivor who has transformed pain into power, fear into fortitude. And as I tread the path of self-love, I leave footprints of courage, each step a proclamation that, despite the haunted dreams, I am the author of my own triumphant awakening.

—In the haunting depths of my night, I confront the spectre of a past that stains my dreams.

Perseverance

The dawn of each new day heralds the initiation of a sombre verse, a melancholic sonnet of despair where shadows pirouette to the discordant rhythm of life's relentless blows. It seems as if the universe, in an orchestrated malevolence, conspires with cosmic forces, hurling tempestuous storms my way with a cruel insistence, threatening to erode the very bedrock foundations of my being.In the symphony of my existence, where every week unfolds as a haunting melody composed of dissonant notes, each day resonates with a relentless crescendo of hardship that lays heavy upon the fragile strings of my soul.Within this cosmic turbulence, my soul, once a vibrant blossom in the garden of existence, now resembles a wilted flower ensconced in a perpetually twilight-kissed field. The weight of unyielding darkness, like a shroud, envelopes my essence, and the tendrils of despair unfurl like tendrils of creeping ivy, ensnaring the delicate tendrils of my spirit. The persistent struggle becomes palpable as my soul, battered and bruised, strains under the gravitational pull of adversity.

In the face of this impending collapse, I clutch at distractions as if they were fragile lifelines, intricately weaving illusions of normalcy to shield myself from the encroaching darkness. These illusions, delicate as gossamer threads, cast a fragile veneer upon the surface of my reality, concealing the profound turmoil that simmers beneath. It is a masquerade, a dance of shadows performed upon the stage of my existence, a desperate attempt to stave off the inexorable descent into the abyss.

In the corners of my mind, a siren song, haunting and beguiling, plays the tempting notes of surrender. The notion lingers in the air like a melancholic aria, whispering that perhaps ending the pain is the only plausible answer, a morose finale to a tumultuous symphony. Yet, amidst this desolate composition, I persist—an unyielding figure amidst the mournful echoes, a lone survivor navigating the heartrending melody.

The resilience I find within the desolation is a testament to the indomitable spirit that refuses to be entirely subdued by the relentless cacophony of life's sorrows. In the midst of the sorrowful echoes, I forge a silent pact with endurance, a covenant with persistence that echoes through the corridors of my being—survival, each note a triumph over the dolorous chords that seek to dominate my existence. And so, in this grand symphony of life, I persist, not as a mere participant, but as a conductor of my own resilience, orchestrating a melody that, against all odds, continues to harmonise with the cadence of my enduring spirit.

—amidst the melancholic sonnet of despair, I persist—a lone survivor navigating the heartrending melody, forging a silent pact with endurance that echoes through the corridors of my being, orchestrating a triumphant symphony of resilience against life's relentless blows.

Industriousness

Embroidered with the intricate threads of endeavour, I traverse a landscape devoid of the privilege of ease. No benevolent hand has bestowed upon me the opulent inheritance of effortless prosperity; instead, I navigate the labyrinth of life with the same perspicacity demanded of every denizen of this terrestrial sphere. I, the architect of my own destiny, find myself toiling relentlessly, unburdened by the elusive elixir of unearned advantage. The crucible of endeavour shapes my every step, and the crucible, it seems, is indifferent to the pedigree of my being. As I labour in the forge of existence, the echoes of meritocracy reverberate through the chambers of my soul, demanding a tithe of diligence comparable to that exacted from all who partake in the grand opera of human toil. There lies no respite, no shelter in the shadows of privilege; rather, I am consigned to the exigency of perpetual exertion, sculpting my narrative in the chisel strokes of tenacity, for in the lexicon of my life, entitlement finds no place, and the burdens of achievement rest squarely upon shoulders fortified by the sweat of endeavour.

—Industriousness is the song of relentless labour, each note a step toward dreams realised; it's the unyielding spirit that turns sweat into golden threads of accomplishment.

Ephemeral Elegance

In the vast expanse of time, I discern an immutable truth: absolute beauty, a profound view with the golden threads of the cosmos, resides in the symphony of every atom and in the minute of moments. As the Earth pirouettes through the seasons, each one unfurls its own opulent canvas—a chiaroscuro of nature's palette, painting the world with the vivid hues of ephemeral grace. Spring, a masterful artist, breathes life into dormant landscapes, coaxing blossoms to unfurl like delicate origami, each petal a testament to the detailed dance of renewal. Summer, with its sun-kissed days, unfolds a verdant melody, where the resplendent foliage sways in the warm embrace of a gentle breeze, and the world becomes a haven of abundance. Autumn, a painter of melancholy, transforms the leaves into a kaleidoscope of warm tones, a bittersweet symphony of letting go. Winter, a sculptor of stillness, blankets the earth in glistening frost, creating a serene tableau of quiet introspection.

Yet, beyond the canvas of nature's grandeur, beauty manifests in the souls of individuals, each akin to a unique flower in the garden of humanity. The human spirit, like the resplendent blooms that grace the landscape, reveals the exquisite intricacies of inner landscapes—a kaleidoscope of emotions, experiences, and aspirations. The laughter of kindred souls echoes like a melodious song, resonating through the corridors of time, weaving a tapestry of shared joy. Even in the face of adversity, the human spirit unfurls, resilient as the blossoms that brave the winds of change, each petal an affirmation of strength and tenacity.

The grandeur of existence, akin to a celestial sonnet, whispers tales of perennial allure, sung by the zephyrs that carry the fragrance of possibility. Amidst the turbulence of life, there exists an ethereal serenity—a sweet melancholy that transcends the transient nature of our mortal coil. Like a solitary poet contemplating the vastness of the cosmos, I find solace in the profound beauty that permeates every facet of our existence. In the sacred dance of life, where every heartbeat is a rhythm and every breath a verse, beauty reveals itself in the poetry of resilience, an eternal ode to the enduring spirit that navigates the ever-shifting currents of time.

—like the fragile petals of a cherry blossom, fleeting and delicate, here one moment and gone the next.

Loss Of Lavender Love

In the dimness of recollection's embrace, lies the shadow of days drowned in the suffocating scent of lavender, where grandmother's arms were but fleeting memories of solace, and her touch a ghostly whisper through the strands of time. In her home, where lavender once bloomed with vitality, now wilted, suffocated by the weight of grief, we sought refuge in the hollow remnants of her love, each wisp of lavender a mocking reminder of what once was. She would weave my hair with delicate fingers, now stilled in eternal slumber, each knot a cruel knot in the unravelling fabric of our shattered existence. In her absence, we are adrift, a fractured family torn apart by the merciless hands of fate, our bonds frayed and fragile, hanging by the thinnest of threads. Our homeland, a desolate landscape of memories, where every footfall echoes with the hollow resonance of loss, every breath tainted by the bitterness of regret. But when she departed, she not only took with her her own light, but she extinguished the flame of my mother's spirit, leaving behind a barren wasteland where joy once flourished. Now, the scent of lavender is not a soothing balm, but a suffocating shroud, each petal a dagger, each stem a reminder of the relentless march of time, carrying us further from the warmth of her embrace. And I, haunted by the relentless spectre of impending sorrow, tremble at the thought of facing a world stripped bare of my mother's presence, knowing the devastation it will bring, for I have witnessed the unravelling of a soul, torn apart like lavender torn from its roots, left to wither and die in the unforgiving embrace of grief.

— Each wilted bloom bears witness to the absence of her nurturing embrace, a silent testament to the irreparable loss that now shadows our fractured existence.

Infinite Homage

He possesses the skill to construct a city, a certain capacity inherent within him. There's a hollow in his chest, a niche waiting to cradle a heart perfectly, and he envisions that if he could only manoeuvre one into place, then the game would be over. He raises the moon on a crane, diligently scrubbing it until it radiates with brilliance.

In exchange, I offer my heart, a contribution to create a space—a testament to a love that surpasses hunger. Know this, if you ever come across these words: there was a time when having you by my side meant more to me than any combination of words, more than all the blue hues in the world. The memory of you will linger, etched in my mind, a touch upon your skin. It will hurt, but it will be my own. Some aspects prove more challenging to articulate than others, a liquid loveliness of words that only half-dawns in comprehension.

I'll embody all the poets, extinguish them, and step into each one's place in succession. Every time love is inscribed in the words of poetry, it will be a homage to you. But you are my nomadic wind, my love wanders freely, touching everything in its path, hoping to find you in the whispers of the breeze.

—I pretended I knew the way. Especially when our love angel unleashed one day.

Integral Reflections
A Passage

In the expanse of my emotions, love is an undivided terrain, a sentiment woven seamlessly into the fabric of my being. I don't entertain the notion of fragmented affection, for my soul, by its very nature, is predisposed to an all-encompassing depth. There exists within me a habitual dreaminess, a restlessness that springs not from a lack of intelligence, but from the essence of my disposition. Someday, I intend to unravel the intricacies within, to articulate those aspects of myself that remain enigmatic. When I immerse myself in the pages of a book, it becomes a solitary dialogue. I critique, scrutinise, discern its faults and virtues, spiralling into thoughts so profound that I lose myself in the labyrinth, grappling with understanding. My approach to literature deviates from the conventional; I engage deeply, play with its nuances, exploring the uncharted territories of my thoughts. I often find myself contemplating things that transcend the realm of reality, and as I navigate this intricate dance, I realise the divergence from a simpler, more innocent engagement with life. The mysteries of existence beckon, and in my unique introspection, I discover a landscape rich with complexity and unexplored dimensions.

—love flows as an indivisible stream, intertwining seamlessly with the essence of my existence.

Emulated Essence

In the ritual of drawing upon the acrid tendrils of smoke, a tacit covenant transpires with momentary solace, a communion with the deceptive allure of cigarettes. Their ephemeral warmth envelops, a veiled refuge concealing the struggles within. Despite earnest vows to sever ties, the haunting echoes of craving persist—a tenacious tether to the familiar dance of addiction. Withdrawal, an intimate pain, unfolds as a visceral battle waged within, shadows etched in the delicate neural pathways. The nicotine's whispers, a beguiling lure, beckon in silent yearning, a clandestine embrace of escape. The journey to quit unfolds as a cyclical landscape, punctuated by relapses—a dance with an erstwhile lover, a bittersweet reunion. Yet, each drawn breath carries the weight of heartbreak, an acknowledgment of surrender to shadows and a fateful tryst with the ever-lingering spectre of mortality. The rhythm of quitting, a staccato beat, weaves a symphony of struggle—an uphill climb in the ceaseless battle against the seductive dance of smoke. In the haze, a tale of heartbreak unfolds—a journey to quit, a vessel set to sail, and in the quiet moments, an unspoken resilience to heal, a story whispered but untold, echoing through the corridors of time

—It's the elusive fragrance lingering in the air, evoking memories of forgotten dreams and untold tales of longing and nostalgia, like a fleeting glimpse of a distant star, it beckons from the depths of the heart, a beacon of inspiration guiding us through the boundless realms of imagination.

Temporal Reflections
A Chronological Tribute

In an alternate cosmos, my window is agape, and I recline upon my floor. A mere five years mark my existence, a time untouched by sorrow's breath. The innocence of youth envelops me, a sanctuary of untainted dreams where nothing bad has befallen my tender heart.

Yet, across the river of time, the current inexorably flows. It carries me away from that window, from the blissful moments of unspoiled joy. The waters, once serene, now ripple with the echoes of life's intricacies. Nature's hand has moulded the stream, leaving behind the vestiges of change.

As I stand at the banks of remembrance, gazing upon the familiar waters, I realise that I am no longer the same, and neither are the currents I left behind. The river, though it may wear the semblance of familiarity, is an altered flow, shaped by the passage of time and the touch of life's elements.

Returning, it becomes evident that what appears unchanged is, in essence, a different river. The echoes of laughter and the whispers of innocence, though imprinted in the waters, are subtly transformed. I am now a different person, bearing the imprints of a journey through unfamiliar tributaries.

Thus, I comprehend the immutable truth: you cannot traverse the same river twice. In that parallel existence, my window is open, and I lie upon my floor, aged a mere five. Yet, in this universe, shadows have touched my past, shaping the riverbanks of my soul, and sculpting a narrative that echoes through the ages.

—I am forever transformed by the passage of time, a testament to the ever-evolving chronicles of life's journey.

Inscrutable Soliloquies

In the realm of our personalities, we each harbour an unsocial, taciturn disposition, reluctant to voice our thoughts unless we anticipate uttering words that will captivate the entire room. Am I an individual or merely a collection of poems about love and grief, bound together like pages within a tome? Poetry endures because it possesses the power to haunt, an enigma that thrives in the liminal space between utter clarity and profound mystery. It resists complete comprehension, defying exhaustion, persisting as a force that lingers, leaving an indelible mark on the echoes of our existence.

—Like elusive echoes in the night, these inscrutable murmurs defy interpretation, weaving of mysteries that elude the grasp of understanding.

Synchronicity

Love, in its essence, has never been a source of fear or wrongness; rather, it has been the locus where I seamlessly belong. The integration of another into the fabric of my being is an unfamiliar terrain, an uncharted intimacy. What truly holds significance is life itself—the ceaseless journey of discovery, an everlasting and perpetual process that transcends the mere exploration of love. In a moment of intimate expression, I convey to him, "Should you ever embrace the passage of time with love, extend an invitation to me. I would willingly relinquish the weariness of my bones to craft tea for you and recite poetry." In that instant, he observes me with eyes that possess an unnerving loveliness, a subtle amusement playing upon his features. It is as if he comprehends the profound effect he exerts upon those fortunate enough to be ensnared by his presence.

—— Where fate and fortune twine their melodies, there exists a dance of serendipity—a harmonious convergence of moments, where cosmic threads weave together in perfect unity. It's the whispered language of the universe, where chance encounters and aligned destinies paint the canvas of life with strokes of synchronicity, revealing the interconnectedness of all things.

Equilibrium

I traverse a nuanced terrain where the sombre silhouettes of systemic inequities cast a pervasive pall. As a woman of colour, the struggle becomes an understated melody in the symphony of daily life, akin to the resonant undertones of a profound concerto. Within this dynamic choreography, resilience emerges as the leitmotif, a forceful melody that reverberates through the steps of my journey. Picture me as an unwavering figure, akin to a phoenix ascending from narratives of suppression, challenging the entrenched norms that seek to circumscribe my identity. The dialogues we exchange, a collective discourse against oppressive structures, echo with the robust harmonies of unity, a sisterhood woven with threads of mutual understanding and empowerment.

We stand united as a constellation of voices, defying the gravitational pull of discrimination, be it based on gender or ethnicity. In the garden of diversity, seeds of transformation are meticulously sown, blossoming into a rebellion characterised by exquisite beauty and transformative vigour. Our laughter, a radical counterpoint, defies the prescriptive expectations imposed upon us, forging a path where resilience and empowerment intertwine like the most intricate lacework. Within this narrative, envision me as a resolute protagonist, navigating the complexities with a countenance etched in unwavering determination, fostering a revolution marked by profound acceptance, love, and an unassailable sense of pride.

—We weave a narrative of transformation, sowing seeds of unity and empowerment in the garden of diversity, crafting a harmonious rebellion against oppression's discordant chords, where harmony emerges from the interplay of chaos and order.

Indomitable Fortitude

Within the crucible of adversity, I cultivate a resilience so intricately forged that it resembles the fine craftsmanship of shadows, weaving a tapestry of fortitude against the backdrop of life's storms. A solitary vessel, my spirit sails resolutely through the turbulent waves, seeking refuge in the unwavering embrace of stoicism—a bastion of tranquillity amidst the chaos.

Emotions, once vibrant blooms adorning the garden of my soul, now resemble withered petals, their once-splendid hues faded by the relentless passage of time. Swept away by the bitter winds of experience, they become poignant relics of a garden long forgotten—an Eden where the echoes of laughter once reverberated with the carefree joy of yesteryears. In the echoes of my laughter, a silent strength emanates, constructing a stoic fortress that stands impervious against the erosive currents of time, resilient as ancient stone weathered by the ages.

Yet, in my unyielding stance, I morph into a forlorn statue, a solitary figure cast amidst a garden of tears. This tear-stained landscape, an intricate mosaic of sorrows, remains untouched by the delicate rain that nourishes the vibrant blooms of joy. As stoicism, my loyal companion, shields me from the tempest's gale, I find myself marooned in the desolate expanses of emotional solitude—a survivor of storms, with no oasis of solace visible on the horizon.

The paradox unfolds: stoicism, my silent ally, serves as both a sturdy vessel navigating the tumultuous seas and an isolating force, rendering me a solitary sentinel in the melancholic garden of tears. The delicate balance between resilience and isolation creates a poignant tableau—a narrative etched in the lines of fortitude and the poignant echoes of laughter that once danced among the vibrant blooms of joy. Thus, I remain, a stoic voyager, weathered yet unbroken, sailing through the boundless expanse of life's tempests, seeking solace in the fragments of beauty that endure amidst the tears.

—stoicism stands as a beacon of tranquility, where weaving fortitude blooms .A refuge amidst the chaos, crafting resilience from the echoes of laughter and tears.

Enigmatic Reverberations

In the quiet spaces between these lines, I want you to understand that there existed a time when your presence was more coveted than the resonance of any uttered words. More valued than the vast expanse of cerulean stretching across the world. Love, a mirage that dances on the edges of perception, I'd willingly surrender to its illusion if only belief would anchor it in reality. Yet, everything now wears the shroud of distance, draped in a sombre hue like shale at the canyon's depths or basks in the warmth of proximity, unthinking like the blossoms of a pink dogwood tree. There's an intimacy, a taming of our essences, a profound connection coursing through our veins in the midst of this metaphorical forest. The weight of gratitude echoes in repeated phrases, a reminder that I owe, that my steps are stained with my own struggles. The offer lingers, a generous hand extended, asking for desires yet unspoken. Others around us bear the weight of weariness, and I yearn to extend a comforting embrace, to speak gentle words into the tired echoes of their souls. There's an internal conflict, a hesitation born from the fear of untamed impulses, never certain whether sanity or chaos governs my intentions. In this tumultuous canvas of existence, where light refracts and paint remains steadfast, I grapple with the question of fidelity, wondering what it means to be true when everything is in constant flux.

—know that once your presence eclipsed the resonance of spoken words and the expanse of cerulean skies. Love, a captivating illusion, teeters between belief and reality, as distance shrouds everything in sombre hues or bathes it in the warmth of closeness.

Whispers in the Steam
Brewing Love's Elixir

I find solace in the ritual of brewing tea, where each delicate gesture becomes an ode to our intertwined souls. The teapot, a vessel of serenity, whispers secrets of affection as it cradles the fragrant leaves within its embrace. With each measured pour, I imbue the liquid with the warmth of my devotion, watching as it unfurls in the cup like petals of a sorrowful bloom. The aroma, a symphony of fragrances, dances through the air, weaving tales of longing and tenderness that linger in the recesses of my mind. In the gentle swirls of steam rising, I see reflections of our shared moments—moments of laughter, of whispered confessions, of silent understanding. For in the steaming depths of this elixir, I find refuge from the tempests of the world, a sanctuary where love's tender embrace envelops me in its gentle caress.

And though distance may stretch our hearts across vast oceans, I will make him tea, for its warmth and comfort mirror the depths of his own soul, a beacon of solace in the darkness of our longing. With each sip, I am transported to the warmth of his embrace, to the safety of his presence, to the quietude of our shared dreams. And as the tea leaves settle at the bottom of the cup, I am reminded of the transient nature of our love—fragile yet resilient, fleeting yet eternal. So I will continue to brew tea, to pour out my heart in each cup, knowing that in its comforting embrace, I will always find a piece of him, a fragment of our love that transcends time and distance.

—Amidst gentle swirls of rising steam, reflections of shared moments emerge, offering sanctuary from life's tempests, where love's embrace envelops me in its gentle caress, bridging the distance across vast oceans with each comforting sip.

The Elusive Alchemy of Self in Artistic Creation

Within the appearances, there persists a prevalent belief that acquiring my shoes, donning my dress, or mimicking the strokes of my makeup artist will seamlessly replicate my narrative. Yet, the alchemy woven into these moments remains elusive to those who aspire to mirror my allure. Unbeknownst to them, I am not innately beautiful; my semblance as such is fleeting and selectively conjured. The awareness of causing pain, a discomfort that pierces through, is a weight too heavy to bear. The consciousness of its necessity creates a dissonance, an incongruity that I find burdensome. In the realm of artistic creation, it's not the miraculous sprouting of a seed that captivates, but the revelations of oneself embedded within the woven fabric of one's own work. The labour of the creator, the source from which creation emanates, eludes the contours of affection. The adoration is reserved for the reflection of oneself mirrored in the artist's creation. It's not the miracle of creation itself but the recognition of one's essence encapsulated within that holds sway. Amidst the artistic endeavour, the desire for a crafted portrait emerges—a vessel capturing one's essence, an emblem of the perpetual quest for self-reflection.

—My beauty is transient and selectively conjured, burdened by the awareness of causing discomfort and the dissonance of its necessity, while in artistic creation, it's not the seed's sprouting but the revelations embedded within one's own work that captivate, where adoration is reserved for the reflection of oneself mirrored in the artist's creation.

Inferiority Complex

I find myself ensnared in the web of fear, a sprawling expanse woven from the threads of past failures and whispered doubts that have haunted me since the tender days of youth. From the earliest whispers of ambition, I have felt the weight of expectation settling upon my shoulders like an ancient burden, pressing down with a force akin to the weight of Atlas's celestial sphere. In the tapestry of my mind, I have meticulously crafted a facade of perfection, each delicate stitch concealing the fractures beneath, lest the world glimpse the vulnerability that lies within.

Imposter syndrome, that insidious serpent, coils around my consciousness, its venomous whispers poisoning my sense of self-worth and leaving me adrift in a sea of doubt. I am a marionette, dancing to the tune of societal expectations, my every movement a carefully choreographed performance designed to maintain the illusion of competence and confidence. Yet beneath the veneer of composure lies a heart that trembles with the fear of inadequacy, haunted by the spectre of failure that lurks in the shadows of my mind.

As I journey through the corridors of memory, I am confronted by the ghosts of my past, each failure a phantom that looms large in the recesses of my consciousness, a constant reminder of the fragility of my aspirations. I have watched as those around me stumbled and fell, their dreams shattered like glass against the unyielding stone of reality, and I have felt the chill of apprehension seeping into my bones, knowing that no matter how diligently I toil or how fiercely I strive, there is always the possibility of defeat.

And so I tread carefully, tiptoeing along the razor's edge of ambition, my every step fraught with the fear of stumbling and falling into the abyss of disappointment. Yet amidst the darkness that threatens to engulf me, there flickers a glimmer of hope, a fragile beacon of resilience that refuses to be extinguished. For even in the face of adversity, I cling to the belief that within the crucible of failure lies the seed of growth, and that with each setback, I am one step closer to realising the full extent of my potential.

—doubt, I navigate past failures, clinging to hope's fragile light, knowing growth blooms from adversity's seed.

Inward Spiral

In the silent sanctuary of my mind, where echoes of laughter once reverberated, now reigns a solemn symphony of anguish and despair. Each morning, I awaken to a world painted in hues of sorrow, the weight of leaden skies bearing down upon me like a suffocating shroud. Bound by invisible chains of anxiety and despair, I find myself imprisoned within the confines of my own bed, unable to break free from the relentless grip of my own thoughts. My room, once a bastion of solace and serenity, now stands as a haunting reflection of the turmoil within—a chaotic landscape littered with the detritus of my shattered dreams and fractured psyche.

Some days, reality is a twisted kaleidoscope of shifting hues, where the boundaries between fantasy and truth blur into indistinct shades of grey. I reach out to grasp at the fragments of certainty, only to find them slipping through my fingers like grains of sand. Other days, the world is a canvas splattered with vibrant splashes of anxiety, each stroke a testament to the tumult that rages within. I am a prisoner of my own mind, trapped within the confines of a labyrinthine maze where every twist and turn leads me further into the depths of despair.

Why must I be shackled to this labyrinth of torment, where every step is a battle against unseen demons? Why could I not have been granted the solace of normalcy, instead condemned to wander these winding corridors of despair? These questions echo endlessly in the recesses of my mind, a relentless refrain that serves only to deepen the abyss of my despair. And yet, amidst the darkness that threatens to consume me, there flickers a glimmer of hope—a fragile ember that refuses to be extinguished. For even in the depths of despair, there lies the promise of redemption, the possibility of finding peace amidst the chaos. And so I press on, clinging to the hope that one day, I will emerge from the shadows and bask in the warmth of the light once more.

—Each dawn heralds a world cloaked in melancholy, as the oppressive weight of leaden skies enshrouds me in its suffocating embrace. Ensnared within the invisible shackles of anxiety and despair, I find myself ensconced within the confines of my own bed, unable to liberate myself from the relentless grasp of my tumultuous thoughts. I am trapped within the labyrinth of my own mind.

Despair's Redemption

Love is a twisted sorrow, woven from the tattered remnants of my shattered innocence. From the earliest whispers of consciousness, I bore witness to the harrowing spectacle of my parents' loveless bond—a bond corroded by the acidic sting of resentment and the suffocating grip of indifference. Their hollow embraces served as a chilling prelude to the desolation that awaited me, a desolation that seeped into the very marrow of my bones, staining my soul with the indelible mark of despair.

Trust, once a fragile beacon guiding me through the darkness, now lies shattered and splintered, fractured by the relentless onslaught of betrayal and abandonment. How can I dare to believe in the possibility of love when all I have ever known is the icy embrace of solitude and isolation? To me, love is a distant dream, its allure tarnished by the bitter taste of disappointment and disillusionment, its promises rendered hollow by the cruel hand of fate.

And yet, amidst the wreckage of my shattered illusions, a solitary tear still glistens—a silent testament to the pain that courses through my veins, a poignant reminder of the wounds that refuse to heal. For even in the deepest depths of despair, there lies a flicker of hope—a fragile ember that refuses to be extinguished. I may stumble and falter along the way, my steps heavy with the burden of my past, but I refuse to surrender to the darkness that threatens to consume me. For I am determined to carve out a sliver of light amidst the shadows, to reclaim my own narrative and forge a new path towards redemption and healing, even as the echoes of my past continue to haunt me with their mournful lament.

—Love, once a guiding light, now a labyrinth of sorrow; trust shattered, leaving me adrift in a sea of disillusionment.

Threshold of Potential

The seeds of personal evolution often find purchase amidst the fertile soil of discomfort, where the verdant tendrils of change unfurl amidst the labyrinthine roots of uncertainty. As a humble scribe traversing the vast expanse of literary expression, I can but offer a guiding beacon, illuminating the path ahead, cognizant that the odyssey itself is a solitary sojourn. There exists no assurance of placid seas or idyllic denouements; rather, each diurnal cycle presents an exigent quandary—to linger in the familiar embrace of stasis or to embark upon the untrodden path of exploration. The morrow, ensconced within the nebulous veil of temporality, holds no covenant of certitude. Hence, upon this auspicious juncture, I extend a gracious entreaty—a call to unlatch the portals of possibility and traverse the threshold of potentiality. However, it is incumbent upon you, dear voyager, to summon the requisite fortitude to traverse that inaugural step—to embrace the discomfort inherent in growth and the nebulous enigma of the expedition ahead.

For too protracted a duration, we have languished within the secure enclave of the familiar, content to ensconce ourselves within the confines of our comfort zones, wherein the edges are smoothed and the peripheries dulled. Yet, authentic metamorphosis awaits beyond the pale of the known, within the uncharted hinterlands of the unfamiliar, where the terrain is rugged and the vista obscured by the umbral spectres of obscurity. It is here, amidst the maelstrom of uncertainty, that we unearth the true mettle of our fortitude and the depths of our latent potential.

Yet, the embarkation upon this prodigious journey necessitates a willing submission to discomfort—to confront the abyssal chasm of uncertainty, to grapple with the trenchant serrations of vulnerability, and to surmount the formidable citadel of change. It is within these crucibles of discomfort that the gemlike truths of our existence are excavated and the dormant reservoirs of our resilience are awakened, forging novel pathways and reshaping the contours of our being.

—Embrace the unknown, summoning fortitude to navigate uncertainty's labyrinth, for therein lies the crucible of growth and the genesis of transformation.

Luminescent Reverie

The ethereal beams of sunlight, imbued with a mystical allure, weave their luminous tendrils into the recesses of my frostbitten heart, suffusing it with a gentle warmth that defies reason. It is a curious paradox that these seemingly inconsequential rays of light, so insignificant in their individuality, hold sway over the vast expanse of my daydreams, casting a luminous halo upon the otherwise mundane fabric of existence. How irrational it seems, yet how profound is the wellspring of joy that springs forth from the simple desire to be liked and loved, to bask in the warmth of affection bestowed upon us.

And yet, it is not solely the sun's radiance that stirs the depths of my soul; for when the moon, resplendent in its full glory, casts its silvered gaze upon the world, its influence is manifold. It is a force that transcends mere illumination, permeating our dreams with its silken touch, stirring the embers of our inner lunacy, and exerting a subtle yet profound influence upon the delicate balance of our nervous systems. In its luminous embrace, we are drawn into a dance of light and shadow, where reality melds with fantasy, and the boundaries between dream and waking life blur into indistinct shades of ambiguity.

And in those fleeting moments of reverie, when I lay down my pen and surrender myself to the whims of imagination, I find solace in the imagined embrace of your hands—your fingers interlaced with mine, a tangible testament to the unyielding bond that binds us together. It is a gesture both intimate and profound, a silent vow of fidelity that transcends the confines of mere words. For even if my hand were to be wrenched from its socket, I would not relinquish my grasp, holding fast to the fragile thread of connection that binds us together in an unbreakable bond of love and devotion.

— while the moon's silvered gaze stirs the embers of my soul, blurring the lines between reality and fantasy.

Linguistic Chasm

I find myself drifting, a ghostly figure amid the bustling world of the living. There was a time when I danced in harmony with the rhythms of life, when my presence was palpable and my voice resonated with laughter. Yet, as the days passed, a silent chasm widened between me and those I held dear, a linguistic barrier that severed the threads of connection that once bound us together. One fateful dawn, I awoke to find that our languages no longer intertwined, our words lost in translation, our hearts adrift in separate currents. Despite my desperate attempts to grasp their new dialect, to decipher the cryptic codes of their expressions, I found myself condemned to the outskirts of their existence, a mere observer in the theatre of their lives. No matter how ardently I pursued comprehension, how fervently I sought reconciliation, the gap between us remained insurmountable, an unbridgeable expanse that stretched into the abyss of uncertainty. I linger on the fringes of their consciousness, a shadowy spectre haunting the periphery of their awareness, a silent witness to their joys and sorrows. While they forge ahead, forging new connections and weaving new narratives, I am left stranded in the hinterlands of solitude, a solitary voyager navigating the uncharted depths of isolation. Oh, how I yearn to reclaim my place among them, to once again share in their joys and sorrows, but alas, I am condemned to wander the desolate landscapes of estrangement, a ghost in the lives of those I once held dear.

—once harmonising with life's rhythms, now lost in a silent chasm of linguistic separation.

Sacred Sacrifice

I languish, ensnared in the web of my own aspirations for corporeal perfection, relinquishing sustenance in a misguided quest for an ephemeral ideal. With each passing day, I forfeit sustenance as an offering to the altar of vanity, sacrificing the vitality of body and soul upon the altar of societal expectations. I meticulously tally the caloric toll of each forsaken meal, my psyche shackled to the relentless pursuit of an unattainable silhouette, oblivious to the erosion of my own essence. In the merciless gaze of the looking glass, I confront a spectre of myself, a gaunt visage haunted by the absence of nourishment, hollowed by the relentless pursuit of an illusory aesthetic. I believed myself the master of my fate, wielding control over flesh and bone, yet in the throes of my fixation, I found myself ensnared within the tendrils of my own obsession, consumed by the very shadows I sought to evade. Each pound shed marks not only a physical diminishment but a spiritual decay, as laughter fades and joy recedes into the abyss of my deprivation. Amidst the ruins of my desolation, I yearn to awaken from this sombre reverie, to reclaim the vitality I've squandered in the pursuit of an unattainable mirage. Yet, ensnared within the labyrinth of my own making, I fear I have strayed too far from the path of redemption, consumed by the voracious hunger that threatens to devour my very essence until naught remains but the hollow echo of a life once lived.

—I sacrifice sustenance to societal standards, tallying each forsaken meal with a relentless pursuit of an unattainable silhouette. Yet, in the merciless gaze of the looking glass, I confront a spectre of myself, hollowed by obsession, consumed by shadows.

Tribute To Palestine

In the echoes of ancestral winds, my heart beats with the rhythm of Algerian sands, a silent witness to the sorrow etched in the Palestinian sky. Palestine, a second homeland, a kindred spirit painted with hues of struggle and resilience, where every olive tree bears witness to tales of heartache. The landscape echoes a symphony of pain, a requiem for a nation in perpetual mourning. The tears of the Palestinian people, a river of sorrow mirroring the desolation of my own soul.

As an Algerian, the echoes of oppression reverberate through the collective memory, a shared narrative with the Palestinian brethren. We, too, danced beneath the weight of colonial chains, our land soaked in the tears of a battle for liberation against the French. The shackles of oppression became a heavy cloak, a garment woven with threads of anguish and despair. Yet, from the ashes of our shared tribulations, we emerged, a testament to the indomitable spirit that refuses to be extinguished.

In the shadow of oppression, the resilience of the Palestinian people becomes a poignant sonnet, a reflection of the Algerian spirit that once yearned for freedom. The Palestinian sky, like our Algerian sky, has borne witness to the cries of the oppressed, a canvas painted with the hues of shared anguish. The walls that divide them, a sombre echo of the barriers we once faced, stand tall, bearing the weight of a struggle for sovereignty.

As the rivers of time flow, there's a whisper of hope resonating through the Algerian breeze, a tale of escape and emancipation. The footprints of our liberation become guiding stars, illuminating a path where the Palestinian spirit may find solace. In this shared struggle, where the saddest symphonies meld, may the echoes of liberation resonate from the Casbah to the heart of Palestine, reminding the world that resilience and hope persist even in the darkest corners of history.

—From the river to the sea, Falasteen will be free.

About the Author

Tasnim Bensaci, a distinguished Canadian-Algerian poet who stands as a luminous figure in the literary landscape, recognized by her peers for her profound poetry that serves as a captivating reflection of her multifaceted identity and experiences. Born at the intersection of cultures, her life's narrative unfolds a biography, interwoven with the threads of heritage, resilience, and an unwavering love for the art of expression.

From an early age, Tasnim found solace and joy in the written word. Growing up in the richness of Canadian-Algerian heritage, she discovered the power of language to bridge worlds, expressing the nuances of her cultural duality. Writing became not only a means of communication but a deeply personal journey—a dance of pen on paper, translating the whispers of her soul into verses that resonated with authenticity.

Writing is not merely an artistic pursuit; it is an integral part of her daily life—a ritual that brings order to chaos, clarity to confusion, and beauty to the mundane. Her journey as an author is marked by a relentless commitment to the craft, where every stanza is a deliberate act of creation, and every line is a testament to the ceaseless exploration of the human experience.

As an advocate for the transformative power of poetry, Tasnim endeavours to create a space where shared experiences intertwine, forming a collective understanding. Her writings are not only an expression of self but also a communal mirror, reflecting the diverse narratives that enrich the human textile.

www.ingramcontent.com/pod-product-compliance
Lightning Source LLC
Chambersburg PA
CBHW032146040426
42449CB00005B/416